TAMPA BAY
BUCCANEERS

RICHARD RAMBECK

CREATIVE ⓒ EDUCATION INC.

Published by Creative Education, Inc.
123 S. Broad Street, Mankato, Minnesota 56001

Designed by Rita Marshall

Cover illustration by Lance Hidy Associates

Photos by Allsport USA, Bettmann Archives, Duomo, Spectra-Action,
Sportschrome and Wide World

Library of Congress Cataloging-in-Publication Data

Rambeck, Richard.
  Tampa Bay Buccaneers/Richard Rambeck.
  p.cm.
  ISBN 0-88682-385-4
  1. Tampa Bay Buccaneers (Football team)—History. I. Title.
796.332'64'0975965—dc20   90-41210
                                      CIP

Western Florida is one of the fastest-growing areas in the United States. Much of that growth is concentrated around Tampa Bay, one of the busiest harbors in the country. Tampa Bay is surrounded by two major cities —Tampa on the east side of the harbor and St. Petersburg on the west side. Tons and tons of goods are shipped into and out of Tampa Bay, often to other countries. The trade that goes through the harbor and the business generated by this trade account for the rapid growth of Tampa and St. Petersburg. Currently, there are almost two million people living in the Tampa Bay area.

The Bucs continue to bring down opponents.

*Defensive end Lee
Roy Selmon was the
number one pick
overall in the
college draft.*

The National Football League noted the rising population around Tampa Bay and decided to expand to western Florida in 1976. The team is based in Tampa, but is called the Tampa Bay Buccaneers, making it the only franchise in the NFL named for a body of water.

The Tampa Bay Buccaneers played their first season in 1976, and the fans had high hopes for their team. The ownership of Tampa Bay came right out and stated the goal of the team: to be successful as quickly as possible. So the Bucs hired a coach who had never known anything but success. His name was John McKay, and he was one of the most successful college football coaches in history. McKay's team, the University of Southern California Trojans, had great records every year in the 1960s and the first part of the 1970s. While McKay was at USC, the Trojans won nine conference championships, five Rose Bowls, and four national championships. McKay didn't know how to lose, but he would learn very quickly.

When McKay was hired by Tampa Bay, he announced that he had a five-year plan to make the Bucs great. "It's simple," he said, when asked why he had decided on a five-year plan. "I had a five-year contract. If I had a six-year contract, I would have had a six-year plan." McKay knew the Bucs would be losers in the beginning, but even he had no idea how bad they would be. In 1976, Tampa Bay became the only team in modern NFL history to lose every game in a season. The Bucs went 0-14, a record that included a loss to the other first-year NFL team, the Seattle Seahawks.

"We have a lot of rookies and new players," McKay commented after the 1976 season. "It's going to take some

James Wilder, the Bucs' all-time leading rusher.

The Bucs selected USC's star running back Rickey Bell as their first draft pick.

time before we work together as a unit. Just be patient. We'll turn this thing around. The wins will come. Let's just try to improve a little bit every game."

During the 1977 season, it appeared that the Bucs might never win a game, and McKay was wondering if he had forgotten how to coach a winner. In sixteen years at USC, McKay lost only forty games; as the Tampa Bay coach, he lost his first twenty-six games. Everybody made fun of the lowly Bucs. Finally, though, Tampa Bay put it all together. The team lost the first twelve games of the 1977 season, but things changed dramatically in the thirteenth game. The Bucs blitzed the New Orleans Saints 33-14. The following week, Tampa Bay won in front of the home folks for the first time, beating the St. Louis Cardinals 17-7. McKay's five-year plan was starting to work. It had also produced the team's first star.

SELMON IS A HIT ON DEFENSE

When McKay was named Tampa Bay's coach, he said the team's number one priority in its first college draft was to get the top defensive player. The Bucs had the first pick in the 1976 draft, and they used it to take Oklahoma University defensive end Lee Roy Selmon. The first time Selmon walked onto the Tampa Bay practice field, it was obvious that he was one of the best players at his position to come into the league in years.

Lee Roy Selmon grew up on a forty-acre farm near Eufaula, Oklahoma. There were nine Selmon kids, and they all helped out on the farm. Lee Roy and his brother Dewey, the two youngest children in the family, were always big for their age. Older brother Lucious, who played at Oklahoma, always told the coaches there about his two younger brothers, who were already bigger than he was. By the time Lee Roy and Dewey entered high school, they were each six feet tall and weighed about two hundred pounds each. The Selmon family had saved the biggest for last.

Like their brother Lucious, Lee Roy and Dewey Selmon eventually enrolled at Oklahoma. In the four years they were in school, Oklahoma lost only two games. The highlight of this period was when the Sooners won the national championship in 1975. That same year, Lee Roy Selmon was named the nation's top college defensive lineman. McKay knew Tampa Bay had to have Lee Roy Selmon. Actually, the Bucs wound up with both Lee Roy and Dewey; after Lee Roy was picked first in the draft, Tampa Bay used its second-round choice to take Dewey, a linebacker.

When Lee Roy entered pro football, he found that for the first time in his life, he wasn't the biggest guy around. Selmon was six feet three and weighed 255 pounds, which was about average for an NFL defensive end. Lee Roy's size was average, but his talent was anything but ordinary. "He is so quick and so strong," said Ted Albrecht, an offensive lineman with the Chicago Bears. "During the game, Lee Roy never says a word. He just lines up for every play and then comes whirling in like a tornado. I've been told that if you get him mad, he's almost impossible to block. I'm glad I've never gotten him mad."

But Albrecht was fearful of what Selmon could do, mad or not. Once during a game, Albrecht expressed just how tough it was to play against Selmon. "At halftime, I told the

1 9 7 7

A frustrating streak ended for coach John McKay when the Bucs posted their first victory.

coach my deepest secrets. I said I never wanted to be buried at sea. I never wanted to get hit in the mouth with a hockey puck. And I didn't want to go out and play that second half against Lee Roy Selmon."

Few offensive linemen did want to play against Selmon. Soon he was considered one of the top linemen in pro football. He was named to play in several Pro Bowls, and in one, he showed just how good he was. In the Pro Bowl played after the 1981 season, Selmon sacked the quarterback an amazing four times. After he entered the league in 1976, Selmon just got better and better. After twenty-six straight losses in 1976 and 1977, the Bucs started to get better and better, too.

1 9 7 8

Lee Roy Selmon terrorized the opposition as he recorded eleven quarterback sacks.

WILLIAMS WINGS IT IN THE AIR

The improvement took a giant step forward with the draft after the 1977 season. Tampa Bay had the second choice in the 1978 college draft, and the team used it to select Doug Williams, a quarterback from Grambling College in Louisiana. Williams was a classic NFL-type quarterback. He was six feet four, weighed 215 pounds, and had a rocket for an arm. Even in high school, Williams could throw the ball eighty yards in the air.

"Doug had great potential coming out of high school," said Eddie Robinson, who coached Williams at Grambling. "He had size, ability, and, most of all, courage. He would get smashed to the turf over and over, but he'd always get up and do something gutsy. He was one determined athlete." And the Bucs were determined to get Williams.

Even before Williams was drafted, though, there were questions about him. The major consideration, unfortunately, involved his race. Williams was black, and there had been few black quarterbacks in the history of the NFL. Williams shrugged off the question of his color. "Race has nothing to do with what I can and cannot do. I feel I'm a solid pro quarterback who will get better with experience. And whether I'm green, black, purple, or yellow, the only thing that counts is my performance out on the field. I feel confident that when people come to see me perform, they will leave knowing I gave them everything I had." Nothing could be more true.

1 9 7 9

Doug Williams made his mark on the NFL by passing for eighteen touchdowns and over 2400 yards.

McKay left no doubt about Williams's importance to Tampa Bay, calling the quarterback "the future of the franchise." McKay also left no doubt that Williams was Tampa Bay's number one quarterback. "I told him, 'No matter what happens, Doug, you're the quarterback. Nobody's going to come out there and take your place.'"

In 1978, Williams led the Bucs to a 5-11 record. It was a good start to his pro career, but Williams believed he could do better. "I am far from satisfied," he said. "I know both myself and the team can do much better. I'm not out to prove that I can play professional football. I'm out to prove that our team can win championships."

Ahmad Rashad, a wide receiver with the Minnesota Vikings, was one individual who thought he could do it, "Doug Williams is just a super quarterback. He sometimes reminds me of Joe Namath. I would guess that this guy will be the first black quarterback to lead a team to the Super Bowl." In 1979, Williams almost did just that.

The Bucs won the National Football Conference Central Division title in 1979 with a 10-6 record. McKay's five-year plan had taken only four years to produce a champion. And in only his second year in the league, Doug Williams

*Running back
Rickey Bell exploded
for 142 yards and
two touchdowns in
the Bucs' play-off
victory over
Philadelphia.*

had led his team to the playoffs. "I'll always be grateful to Coach McKay for the opportunity he gave me," Williams reflected. "It took guts to make me his quarterback in my rookie year and then stick with me through all the criticism."

McKay said that Williams proved the critics were wrong all along. "People said we couldn't win with a black quarterback," the Tampa Bay coach said. "People said there were 'rumors' about Doug's intelligence. The rumors were wrong. He's a smart young man."

Thanks to Williams's leadership on offense and a defense keyed by Lee Roy Selmon that gave up the fewest yards and the fewest points in the entire NFL, the Bucs were the darlings of the Tampa Bay area. Only two years before, the Bucs had been the joke of the football world. Now after Tampa Bay won the Central Division title, the fans held up signs that said, "From Worst to First." But the team wasn't done.

In the first round of the playoffs, the Bucs faced the Philadelphia Eagles. Behind Williams's passing the team moved out to a 17-7 lead. Selmon and the defense protected that lead, and Tampa Bay eventually won 24-17. The Bucs were in the NFC championship game, to be played on their home field. Everyone expected the game against the Los Angeles Rams to be a defensive struggle, and that's just what it was. Tampa Bay's outstanding defense prevented the Rams from scoring a touchdown. It wasn't hard to figure out why: in addition to the Selmons, the Bucs' defense featured tackle Randy Crowder and two outstanding linebackers—David Lewis and Richard Wood. Wood, nicknamed "Batman" because of the way he flew around the field, led the team in tackles virtually every game.

The Bucs celebrate a victory.

Unfortunately for the Bucs, the home team couldn't generate any offense either. Los Angeles managed three field goals and wound up winning 9-0. The Bucs were stopped one victory away from the Super Bowl. From worst to first? The Bucs nearly went from worst to best.

Three of the best! Linebacker David Lewis joined teammates Lee Roy Selmon and Jimmie Giles in the Pro Bowl.

WILDER RUNS, AND RUNS, AND RUNS

The Bucs fell to earth in 1980, finishing 5-10-1. In 1981, they won the Central Division with a 9-7 record, but Dallas beat Tampa Bay 38-0 in the first round of the playoffs. Tampa qualified for the playoffs again in 1982, but lost in the first round—again—to Dallas. This time the score was 30-17. The following year, the Bucs went 2-14, but they lost something more important than a few games: they lost Doug Williams. The talented quarterback signed with the Oklahoma Outlaws of the new United States Football League before the 1983 NFL season started.

But the Bucs also found something in 1983: their next star. His name was James Wilder, and he was a powerful runner who never seemed to get tired. He was six feet three and weighed 225 pounds, although he seemed much bigger than that. Wilder was acquired in 1981 to be a backup. By 1982 he was a starter. In 1983 he led the team in rushing, despite playing much of the year with broken ribs. In 1984 Wilder set an NFL record for most carries in a season with 407. The same year he gained 1,544 yards, easily a Tampa Bay record. He also caught eighty-five passes for 685 yards. In short, he was the Tampa Bay offense.

Some fans worried that Wilder was being asked to do too much; they were concerned that he would get worn out. They obviously didn't know something about James Wilder: he never got tired of working hard. After practice, Wilder was almost always in the weight room, working on his many muscles. Wilder spent all week preparing for the game on Sunday. He wanted to be ready every time the Bucs gave him the ball.

"When my number is called," Wilder said, "it's my turn to make things happen. It's not that much of a load, really. It's not like I'm running the ball thirty times in a row. Sure, I feel aches a little on Sunday night and Monday morning after games. That's why I look forward to running and weightlifting Monday afternoon. I do that, and I start to loosen up."

What made Wilder special was his body, and his strength. In the offseason, Wilder worked as a male model —that is, when he wasn't working out in the weight room. "If anybody could handle the load," said Tampa Bay offensive lineman Steve Courson, "I guess it would be James. Just look at him. He's like a bodybuilder." Guard Sean Farrell agreed with his teammate, "The thing that makes him different is his exceptional strength. He's as strong as anybody on this team."

Because of his strength Wilder was as good at the end of a game as he was at the beginning. "God doesn't make many bodies like that," commented fullback Scott Dierking. "I've never seen a guy who can run the ball forty times and still look as fresh as the rest of us who have done nothing."

Wilder did a lot on the field, but he said little off the gridiron. He let his play speak for him. "If you didn't know James," said Bucs' running back Adger Armstrong, a good friend of Wilder's, "you'd think he was a snob because of

1 9 8 3

James Wilder streaked seventy-five yards for a touchdown against Minnesota—the longest rushing play in Bucs' history.

Punter Chris Mohr, (pages 18–19).   17

the way he carries himself and the fact that he doesn't say much. But once you get to know him, he's just your basic nice guy."

Wilder's actions on the field quickly helped him become one of the top running backs in the NFL. "He's the best back I've seen," said veteran quarterback Steve DeBerg. Unfortunately, Wilder was like a one-man band for the Bucs. When Doug Williams left, it was as if the passing game left with him. Tampa Bay used Wilder for two reasons: first, because he was good, and second, because the team really didn't have any other offensive weapons.

After Wilder's record-breaking year in 1984, John McKay decided to retire. He had taken the team as far as he felt he could. The new coach, Leeman Bennett, vowed to make the Bucs winners again right away. "I expect our team to contend for the NFC Central Division title now, not later," Bennett remarked at the start of the 1985 season. "Man for man, Tampa Bay has the talent to win it all, but this is the NFL. None of the other teams in the league are going to hand us anything. We're going to have to take it, earn it."

What the Bucs wound up earning was a lot of defeats. Tampa Bay finished with the worst record in the NFL in both 1985 and 1986. The 1986 team finished 2-14, which gave the Bucs the first pick in the 1987 college draft. The team also had the first pick in the 1986 draft, and used it to take Auburn University running back Bo Jackson. But Jackson didn't sign with Tampa Bay; instead, he decided to play pro baseball with the Kansas City Royals. Tampa Bay couldn't afford another mistake like that. In 1987 the team and its new coach, Ray Perkins, had their eyes on another player, one that this time they could sign.

1 9 8 5

The Bucs triumphed over Detroit in overtime for the club's second—and only—victory of the season.

TESTAVERDE ANSWERS HIS CRITICS

The Bucs didn't have to look far for their new star. He was playing college ball at the University of Miami, which had produced a couple of pretty good pro quarterbacks in the 1980s: Bernie Kosar of the Cleveland Browns and Jim Kelly of the Buffalo Bills. But experts called Miami's latest quarterback the best of the bunch. They claimed that Vinny Testaverde had Kelly's strength and Kosar's accuracy in throwing the ball. Testaverde was a can't-miss prospect, they said.

For the third straight year placekicker Donald Igwebuike led the club in points scored.

University of Miami Coach Jimmy Johnson would agree with that. Testaverde, who sat on the bench at Miami for three years waiting for Kosar to turn pro, led the Hurricanes to a 21-3 combined record in 1985 and 1986. Strangely, many chose to remember the few games Testaverde lost in Miami rather than all the games he won. In both 1985 and 1986, Miami lost its final game. First, Tennessee beat the Hurricanes 35-7 in the Sugar Bowl at the end of the 1985 season. Then Penn State topped Miami 14-10 in the Fiesta Bowl a year later to win the national championship.

Critics said Testaverde gave away the game by throwing five interceptions. They said the pressure made Testaverde choke. Johnson said that was completely untrue. "He handled the pressure against Oklahoma extremely well—twice," Johnson said of Testaverde's great games against one of college football's best teams. "And he handled the pressure of about a dozen TV games."

The critics didn't know Testaverde. They didn't know that, no matter what's happening, he doesn't panic. Testaverde proved that on, and off, the field. One time, he was

21

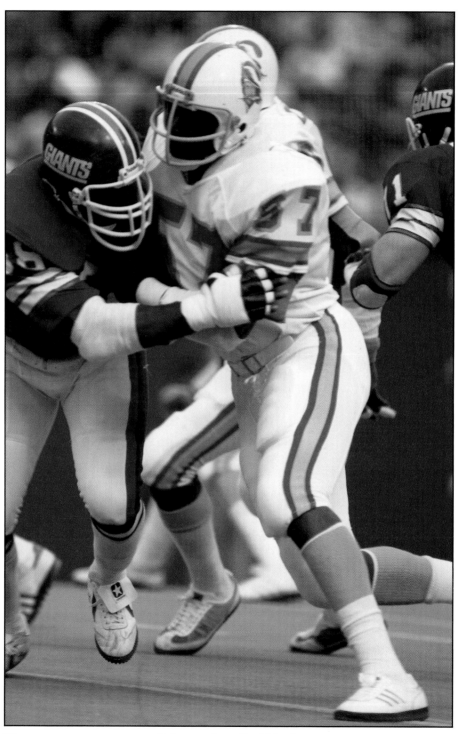

Defense stalwart David Lewis.

on an airplane that was forced to make an emergency landing. A member of the flight crew recognized Testaverde and asked him if he'd help in trying to calm the other passengers. Testaverde did so, gladly. "It was exciting," he remembered. "It sounds weird, but my heart was pounding, and I was into it. It wasn't a scared feeling, but a ready-to-go feeling." This obviously is not a guy who's going to get scared on the football field.

1 9 8 7

Tampa Bay newcomer Mark Carrier ranked first among the NFC's rookie wide receivers.

The Bucs and Coach Perkins didn't listen to the critics. They knew how good Testaverde could be. Tampa Bay drafted the Miami quarterback with the first pick. It was no surprise, particularly because Testaverde and the team had agreed to a contract weeks before the draft. The Bucs were going to pay Testaverde $8.2 million over six years, one of the highest salaries in the NFL. Because Perkins wasn't about to risk the team's investment, he hired the University of Miami quarterback coach, Marc Trestman to help Testaverde get adjusted to pro ball.

But Vinny had more than football on his mind. The first thing Testaverde did after he signed the contract was buy cars for both his parents. "Hey," Testaverde exclaimed, "I owe so much to them. The money is mostly theirs, anyway. Without them, I couldn't have gotten anything."

Testaverde has a habit of being generous to family, friends—and teammates. During his first training camp with the Bucs, Testaverde took fifteen of the veteran players out to dinner, and paid the bill. "I've never seen that done by a rookie," said Scot Brantley, one of the veterans who was treated to dinner. "I thought it was a great gesture on his part."

"Hey," shouted quarterback Steve DeBerg, "he can afford it. But seriously, he hasn't let this thing go to his head,

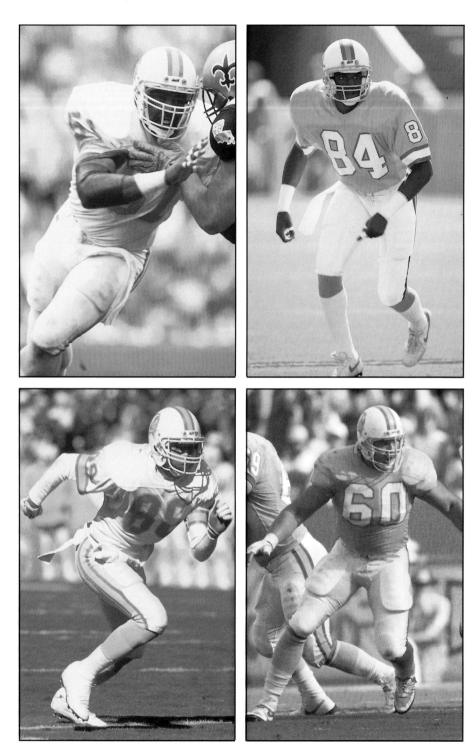

Clockwise: Broderick Thomas, Bruce Hill, Randy Grimes, Mark Carrier.

and he's a very impressive quarterback." DeBerg should know about impressive quarterbacks. He began his career with the San Francisco 49ers and watched the development of another young quarterback, he was named Joe Montana. A couple of years later, DeBerg was playing for the Denver Broncos when they drafted John Elway. If DeBerg is impressed, it really means something.

Testaverde impressed the Bucs with his ability and with his attitude. He worked hard, and he worked long hours. "He signed before the draft," said Bucs' owner Hugh Culverhouse. "He agreed to come and work. He has been around from eight A.M. to five P.M., maybe longer, five or six days a week."

It was soon apparent that Testaverde, a raw rookie, was ready to play in the NFL. "Because of the success he's had, he's gained confidence," said Trestman, the Bucs' quarterback coach at that time. "I think Vinny's been well prepared for the NFL by Miami's offensive system." Trestman knew all about Miami's system; after all, he helped design it.

At the beginning of the 1987 season, Perkins wasn't sure whether Testaverde or DeBerg would start. "I'll start the one who will help us now, but Vinny is our quarterback of the future," he said. Vinny soon became the quarterback of the present as well. DeBerg just couldn't keep Testaverde on the bench, which was a great compliment to Testaverde. As rookies, neither Joe Montana nor John Elway could claim a permanent starting position from DeBerg.

Perkins made Testaverde the top gun, saying he was too good not to use. "Vinny Testaverde should be a great quarterback," Perkins said, "and I don't use the word 'great' too many times." But Testaverde wasn't great at first; in

1 9 8 7

Dazzling debut! Vinnie Testaverde passed for a rookie record 369 yards in his first start.

Former Buccaneer kicker Donald Igwebuike, (pages 26–27).

1 9 8 9

The Bucs' top receiver, Mark Carrier, caught eighty-six passes for over 1400 yards.

fact, he struggled throughout his rookie season. He threw too many interceptions, and Perkin's faith in him was tested. But every time it appeared that Testaverde was headed for the bench, he would rise up and have a great game.

For example, against New Orleans in 1987, Testaverde destroyed one of the best defenses in the NFL. He threw for 486 yards, one of the top passing performances in league history. But Tampa Bay's defense couldn't stop the Saints, who won 44-34. After the game, though, all the Saints could talk about was Testaverde.

Unfortunately, the critics were complaining that the young quarterback made too many mistakes. The Bucs weren't winning, and Testaverde was getting much of the blame. "It's still fun to be me," Testaverde said. "But it's not fun to be me as a football player right now. What would really please me is to go out and play great. That would shut everybody up."

Testaverde was frustrated, but he wasn't discouraged. He knew that the Bucs were still rebuilding. In 1989, the third season at Tampa Bay for both Testaverde and Perkins, things started to come together. Testaverde threw fewer interceptions. And wide receivers Bruce Hill and Mark Carrier had developed into one of the best and most dangerous duos in the NFC.

In addition, the Bucs' defense did not allow nearly as many points in 1989 as it did when Testaverde was a rookie. Rookie linebacker Broderick Thomas showed the most potential of the Bucs' many young defensive players. Perkins was about halfway through a complete rebuilding of the defense, but the young Bucs started to get more and more stingy as the 1989 season went on.

Linebacker William Howard.

The versatile Willie Drewrey.

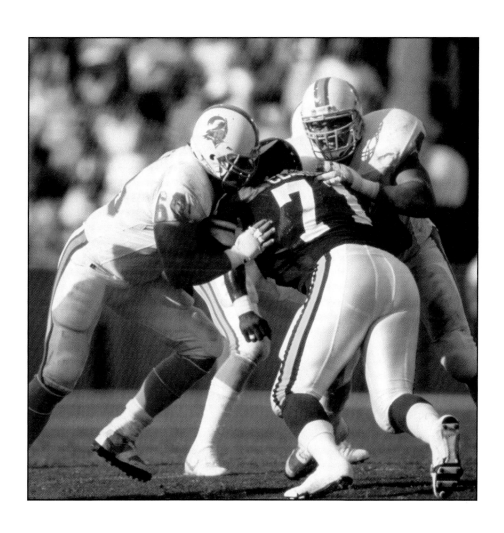

Tampa Bay guard Rick Mallory.

1 9 9 0

Safety Harry Hamilton anchored Tampa Bay's impressive secondary coverage, and fast improving defense.

The Bucs didn't have a winning season in 1989, but they made life miserable for a lot of good teams. Tampa Bay beat the Green Bay Packers in Green Bay, a loss that kept Green Bay out of the playoffs. In the rematch in Tampa, the Bucs lost a heartbreaker on a last-second field goal. Young teams tend to lose close games, and the Bucs were no exception in 1989.

As for Tampa Bay's future, it looks bright—perhaps as bright as it did when Williams and the Selmons were terrorizing the NFC. Ray Perkins has decided to build the team through the draft. As a result, most of the Buccaneers are actually younger than the team's young star, Vinny Testaverde. Perkins also hasn't been afraid to let a veteran player go if it opens up a spot for a promising newcomer.

Ray Perkins knows how to build a winner. He did it with the New York Giants, and he has vowed to do it at Tampa Bay. Some of the ingredients are already in place: Testaverde, Hill, Carrier, running back Lars Tate, and, on defense, Thomas, safety Harry Hamilton, and rookie linebacker Keith McCants, the Bucs' top draft choice in 1990. Although some of these names aren't well known, they soon will be. As the Tampa squad attempts to fight their way to the top of the NFL.